REFLECTIONS ON LOVE AND DISCIPLINE

A Handbook for Parenting Godly Children

Correnna B. Polk

The information provided in this handbook is for informational purposes only and is not intended to be a source or substitute for professional parenting advice.

Scriptures are taken from the KING JAMES VERSION (KJV): KING JAMES VERSION, public domain.

Printed in the United States of America

ISBN 978-0-578-73070-7

JStokes Publishing Company

TABLE OF CONTENTS

Introduction

For many years, I have been inspired to write a book. At first I thought I would perhaps write poetry and songs, but as I observed the world around me in this current generation, I felt a need to share what I have learned over a lifetime about love and discipline as they relate to children.

When I was a child, my mother disciplined me with love; and I am thankful she did because there is no telling what kind of person I would be today if she had not. It is my prayer that parents will learn how to take charge of their children and teach them the importance of respect for themselves and their fellow man, how to dress modestly and speak without using foul language, and how to behave in a decent manner. My mother did that for me, and I am grateful.

I spent most of my child-rearing years as a single parent, and if it had not been for God leading and guiding me, I would not have made it. I married when I was eighteen, and that is when I learned what life was all about. Perhaps I can describe it this way. Monday through Thursday, my husband was fair; but Friday through Sunday he would gamble and drink. When my kids were very small, I often heard, "Mama, I'm hungry," and I often had to reply that Grandma would bring us something to eat after she got off work. Then the three of us would huddle up and go to sleep to escape the gnawing pangs of hunger in our bellies. A meal of cooked bologna and watermelon was not uncommon for us. But even from the time they were small, my children listened to what I taught them, and they allowed the hardships of their youth to shape them into wonderful adults, for which I am thankful.

My son is forty-two years old and, till this day, he respects himself as well as me and anyone else he meets. That did not happen by accident. We will all stray at one point or another, as we are imperfect human beings living in a fallen world, but if we have been brought up to fear and believe in God, we will ultimately return to our training. My son lives the way he was brought up, and I am certain that his Christian upbringing has had a profound effect on the kind of man he has become.

I also have a daughter who died at sixteen. She was a beautiful child who loved the Lord, her family and other people—but that was true in part because I raised her to do so. I firmly believe that, if she were alive today, she would have raised her children the same way she was raised; to fear God and respect others.

In society today, boys' pants are too low, girls' dresses are too short and tight, and foul language is as common as breathing, but sadly these children have few role models and very little instruction. Most of their parents' dress and act the same way. Television as well as all the world around them regularly display immorality and evil. As I watched the effects of all of this on the young people of our nation today, I was inspired not only to think about writing this book, but to actually do it.

Chapter One

The Foundations of Discipline

The primary foundation of discipline must be love. The two go hand in hand—and love is a fruit of the Spirit. In Galatians 5:22-23, we also see several other characteristics that the Spirit produces in us: *"But the fruit of the Spirit is love, joy, peace, longsuffering, gentleness, goodness, faith, Meekness, temperance: against such there is no law."*

If we want to love as the Scripture commands, we need to pay more attention to how we respond to other people's feelings and how we treat them. Love should be unconditional, completely, and absolutely without any reservations. We can all get so wrapped up in ourselves that we become selfish. Before you try to discipline a child, consider how you would feel if you were treated the way you are about to treat your child.

Men, love your family and let them know it. Do not get so involved in your car, boat, fishing trip or whatever other hobby you have that you fail to make time for your spouse and kids. Respond to your family in a kind way. If God has blessed you with a good family or friends, thank Him for that and do everything you can to keep them. Try to make them happy. This is where love comes in, for when you truly love, you do not put anyone or anything else before those you love.

Ladies, I admonish you to do the same. Just love your family. Sometimes, even sensible, hard-working, educated women become so tied up in what is in the house that they do not want their family to leave anything anywhere—or even to lie down or sit on the furniture! Now don't get me wrong. I like the house to be clean and neat but designate somewhere in the house where your family can relax and enjoy themselves. Show more love and understanding. When God gives you a partner, thank God for that man and stop complaining. Kindness tames the beast. You draw more flies with honey than with vinegar. We are all supposed to help one another. I find that most people do better when they are treated with respect. Remember, the three important elements of a happy home are love, education, and discipline. A relationship will work better if you both know God, but even those who do not know God can have good relationships if they employ these elements.

We need to do everything in our power so our children will be the best they can be. Love makes us want the best for our children, but it is impossible to give them the best without morals. How can anyone love or discipline their kids if they themselves are living immorally? God is love, and we must seek to be like Him so that we can love our families as He desires.

Education is also a foundational element of discipline when used the right way. Some have the idea that education makes them better than those who are uneducated, but that is not true. Without knowledge and wisdom from God's Word, it is possible to be an educated fool. If you are educated, acquire knowledge from the Word so that you can use your education wisely.

It is so much easier to teach children about love and discipline if you know the gospel. Children who are being taught about God and how to grow in love and faith will not be ashamed of the gospel of Christ. Even when they stray, this is still the best and right way to teach them.

Parents cannot properly teach a child discipline when they themselves do not understand either love or discipline. I so often see parents that are doing more harm to their children than good. They do not know how to love or discipline their children, and they become jealous if someone else can communicate with their child better than they can. Learning (educating ourselves about) what biblical love is and putting it into practice in our daily lives as we rear our children is paramount if we hope to rear good children. You cannot make anyone love you, but you can love everyone. Being brought up to love others makes all the difference in how we treat each other.

We need to be mindful of the fact that our children need our love, understanding, and discipline the same way we need God's—though we must expect nothing less than respect from them.

I once sold furniture to someone on credit and let that person charge gas on my credit card. They never paid me back and, at first, I was angry. My anger was affecting me to the point where I almost hated that individual, but I prayed and asked God to fill me with love instead. With God's help, my attitude changed and if that person got right, that would be enough payment for me. I had to realize this person needed my forgiveness just as I needed my Heavenly Father's.

It is hard when others treat you wrong—and that's especially true when it's your children. But we still must have love and patience and seek God's strength to endure such evil. Satan is still on the job, but Jesus has already done His job, and that is what counts—because Jesus has all power while Satan has power only over those who disobey God. It is so important for us to remember how much God loves us, and that He loves us so much that He forgives and overlooks our faults. To be like Him, we must do the same; we must give and show a lot of love.

Respect is another important foundational element of discipline. It disturbs me to see abusive parents or disrespectful kids. You see so many out-of-control kids who have no respect for anyone, not even for themselves, which only goes to prove that if you do not respect yourself, you will not respect others. Parents, most teachers are trying to help your children, so stop going to the school and taking sides with your unruly child. In fact, a big part of the problem is that your kids know you are going to head right over to the school and cuss out the teacher - like parent, like child. Instead, be sure your child learns how to spell, read, and write and you will see a world of difference in their attitude.

I do not believe in abusing anything or anyone; there is a huge difference between a spanking and a beating. But you must start disciplining when children are very young. First you must know how to get a child's attention; then you must speak to that child properly—firmly, but with respect. Say what you mean, and mean what you say, and take control. Hug the child and express your love. I know this works, for it worked for my mama when she raised her children, and it worked for me when I raised my children, and it still works today with my great, great nephew and nieces. It is all in how and when you begin training.

When I think back to my own childhood, I love how my mother disciplined me with love and respect. I still wish she had let me learn to style my own hair—and she probably would have if I had asked—because now as an adult I still cannot do anything with it. This is why it is so important to train your children at an early age. The older children become, the harder it is for them to be trained or disciplined.

Love and enjoy each other while you can because there will come a time when you will desire the opportunity to do so, but it will be too late. As we strive to make love the foundation of our relationships, learn how to appreciate one another. Parents, thank your children when they do something nice; children, thank your parents for being good parents and being there when you need them—through good times and bad. Remember that no one is perfect, but we should all be striving for perfection.

The best relationships are built on trustworthiness and honesty. Keep the lines of communication open and work hard to understand each other. Two wrongs don't ever make a right. Parents, know when to keep your mouth closed. Kids, you must sometimes think about what your parents are saying and listen, for your own good.

It is indeed God's will for all of us to discipline our own minds to the best of our abilities, using all the strength He has given to us. Parents must love and train up their children in the way that they should go, and children must listen to and obey their parents. A good parent only wants what is best for their child.

To bring my children up in the right way, I started at an early age spending quality time with them, showing them love, and training them in the way they should go. The early days of a child's life are a critical time for us to bond with them.

It is sad when a parent and child can't get along. I know someone whose daughter is a grown woman with children, and she tells people she hates her mother. They are not speaking to each other, but it started way back when the child was nine or ten, when the mother should have found out what the problem was and worked on repairing the breech between them.

The Powerful Yearning for Love

Children are begging to be loved and disciplined. As my son and I were coming home from church one Sunday, when we got to our apartment, we saw a group of kids hanging around. They started talking to my son about going to church and where they lived. While it was wonderful that they wanted to go to church, it was sad at the same time because their parents should have already had them in Sunday school and morning service. Tragically, they just did not take the time to fulfill their children's needs. I could hear some of their parents cussing and playing loud music while their children were starving for love and discipline. Most of the time when children mimic their parents' ungodly behavior, they are really looking for someone to love them. Yes, a lot of kids are out of control, but whose fault is that? The parents.

Parents, stop using your situation or your children as an excuse not to do your job. While it is God's plan for children to have both parents, many single parents very successfully raise good children. Sure, raising children is a big job, but anything worth doing is going to be a big job. Nothing worthwhile is ever easy. I know that because I am a parent who has done all the things you are finding so hard to do. I am also in school in my sixties. Believe me, it is not easy, but it is possible. I do a lot of praying and ask God to help me and give me more wisdom, more knowledge, and a better understanding. You can do the same when it comes to rearing your children.

Children are so innocent and sweet when they are small. All parents want their child to be the best, but for that to happen, parents must remember that they are responsible to train up that child to love and respect others. It is so sad every time you learn that some child has shot or killed another person; most of the time, it is because the child is out of control. Children say and do whatever they want to because they know the parents are not going to do anything to them. Most of these parents are not failing to discipline out of fear that they will be accused of child abuse; that is just an excuse. It is simply easier for them to let the child do whatever he wants so they do not have to be bothered with him while they are off doing their own thing. I am sure some of these parents really do not know that they're supposed to teach their children at an early age—but in so many cases, they simply don't want to do the hard work of raising kids. Children need a whole lot of love, discipline, and education; they need to be heard and understood. Parents, you must bond with your children when they are young.

If you really do not understand your child after you have done all you can, then get professional help for them. Please help your children to be the best that they can be. Question your kids and find out what is going on in their life and their friends' lives. It is sad to see so many different things on television that kids are doing. You should know when your children are lying, and even when they are not, you should let them know you are there for them.

If you truly love your children, you need to teach them to respect their stepparents, especially if that person is taking care of them financially and treating them right. That deserves respect. Children need to know it is not right to think that being mean to a stepparent will somehow get their own parents back together.

Proverbs 4:1-11 tells us this: *"Hear, ye children, the instruction of a father, and attend to know understanding. For I give you good doctrine, forsake ye not my law. For I was my father's son, tender and only beloved in the sight of my mother. He taught me also, and said unto me, let thine heart retain my words: keep my commandments, and live. Get wisdom, get understanding; forget it not; neither decline from the words of my mouth. Forsake her not, and she shall preserve thee: love her, and she shall keep thee. Wisdom is the principal thing; therefore, get wisdom: and with all thy getting get understanding. Exalt her, and she shall promote thee: she shall bring thee to honor, when thou dost embrace her. She shall give to thine head an ornament of grace: a crown of glory shall she deliver to thee. Hear, O my son, and receive my sayings; and the years of thy life shall be many. I have taught thee in the way of wisdom; I have led thee in right paths."*

So, please, love your children, teach them, and show them that you care. If you do not, you can scar children for life. I know that children want to be loved, just as we all want and need love. If children act like they do not want to be hugged, do not believe that; it is just a shield they've put up to keep from being hurt. In reality, they most certainly want someone to show that they care.

One Sunday I was coming home from church and, as I approached my apartment, some youngsters were sitting on the steps, and I spoke to them. That opened the door, and they started asking me questions about church and telling me why they got out of church. I spent over an hour talking to them, and they appreciated me spending time with them. I mentioned that children want to be loved, and I said some children felt like they were neglected when they were coming up. One of them said that was the way she felt and said it does take a long time to get over it. Parents, some kids never get over it. When I say parents, I am talking to all parents. Treat all children as if they are your own; sometimes you can be a better mentor than their own parents because not everybody knows how to be a parent.

Children, obey adults, especially your parents. Proverbs 20:20 promises, *"Whoso curseth his father or his mother, his lamp shall be put out in obscure darkness."* Ephesians 6 admonishes you in this area as well. Parents, live a respectable life before your children. You can do a world of good for them by the way you live your life—by the way you dress and act. Children do pick up their parents' habits. I am sure you have heard the old saying: *Like mother, like daughter* or *Like father, like son.* So be a good mother for them; insist that they go to school and learn to read and write. You will see a big difference between the behavior of a child that can read and write and one that cannot.

Ask God to help your children and lead them in the right way. Train them up the right way, teaching and telling them about God. Assure them that He is always there to guide them. Encourage them to keep the faith and trust in Him; remind them of His promise that He will direct their path. Prayer is what keeps us in touch with God. Ask God for His help, and He will give it to you. Both children and parents always need God. He watches over us and directs our path. We are in God's hand, and we must put our children in His hand as well. While we cannot live our children's lives for them, we can share God's love with them and provide a foundation for the discipline they need in their lives in order to live a God-honoring life before the Lord.

Practical Applications for Parenting

1. Were you raised with love as the foundation for the discipline you received as a child? If so, give examples of how your parent(s) applied discipline with love. If not, explain how you can demonstrate love differently now with your children when you discipline them.

2. Has there been a time when you have disciplined your child without respecting them? If so, what could you do differently next time?

3. I Corinthians 3:12 refers to the importance of building our lives on the right foundation—like faith, prayer, and Scripture. How can you apply this principle to your parenting to ensure that you lay a good foundation of love and discipline for your child?

Chapter Two

How to Harvest a Disciplined Generation

It is vital to begin teaching our children about God and His love from birth. Take them to Sunday school and church. Do not be reluctant to reprimand them. A good parent tells their children when they are wrong. Because we would like to shield them from everything unpleasant, we try to keep them from making so many mistakes. We do not do this to run their lives like they sometimes accuse us of doing; we are simply trying to give them the benefit of our own experiences.

Every now and then, I watch television talk shows and get so fed up with parents saying they cannot do anything with their teenage children. Perhaps their intentions are good, but as one television host told a parent, you cannot wait until your kids are teenagers to discipline them. It is infinitely better to train them when they are small. Though we might not always know exactly how to solve a problem, the problems are much less complicated when children are young. Children quickly figure out what they can get away with and what they cannot. It is up to us as parents to nip disobedience in the bud quickly, no matter what form it takes. Children want to be loved, and when we discipline them, they will feel more secure in our love even when they are too young to understand why.

We as parents are like farmers, and our children are like the fields. A farmer plows his field and then sows crops of all kinds—corn, cotton, oats, wheat—then he regularly must work the field to keep the crops from being destroyed before the harvest. He destroys the pests that attack the tender plants and clears the grass and weeds out of the way so they don't hinder growth; but depending on the intensity of his efforts, some of the plants survive and some don't. If the farmer has diligently tended his fields, the harvest is typically beautiful and bountiful. But if the farmer has been slothful regarding his care of the tender plants, his field may yield a scanty harvest or even a completely ruined crop.

The parallel with our children is clear. First, we need to carefully plant the seeds of good traits in their lives—seeds of obedience, love, trust, morality, honestly, kindness, loyalty, integrity, respect, and many others. As we tend those plants, some will turn out healthy, some mediocre, and others completely rotten. I will say again that it is not easy being a parent, but regardless of the circumstances, it is our duty to plant, tend and harvest good qualities in our children's lives through love and consistent discipline.

Just like the seeds we plant in a field come from mature plants, I believe children most of the time inherit parental traits (the seed from the mature plant), so it is imperative that we plant good seeds in their lives at a very young age and nurture them faithfully. If the seeds in your own life are not what they should be as an adult, be sure to plant different seeds in your child's life to stop the cycle of unhealthy traits being passed along from one generation to the next.

Here are six seeds you can plant into your children:

1. Train your child to be responsible.

Responsibility applies to many areas. Give your child tasks to accomplish within the family setting and insist that those tasks be accomplished faithfully and fully. When they are not, consequences appropriate to the task should result.

2. Teach your child how to handle money.

You might begin by giving your child an allowance based on work he does around the house. If the job is halfway done, cut the allowance in half. If the work is not done at all, withhold the money.

Teach your child how to divide his earnings into tithe, savings, regular expenses, fun money, etc. When there is enough, help your child open a savings account. Teach your child how to spend money wisely and how to get the best deals on the items he wants to buy. Make sure he understands that he will be better off in a ten-dollar outfit he can pay for than in a thousand-dollar outfit he had to go into debt to buy. Teach him to always pay bills on time. If you instill these behaviors in children when they are small, they will not have any problem continuing these practices as adults.

3. Be respectful and commend your child for a job well done.

When you ask children to do something, do not forget to thank them when they obey. By doing so, you are instilling manners. You would not want anyone hollering or cussing at you; it is inexcusable to treat a child that way. "Do unto others as you would have them do unto you" also applies to us as parents. To get respect, you must give respect; everyone will be happier when this happens.

Remember, you are accountable for your children until they reach eighteen, so exercise your rights as parents and always praise your kids when they deserve it. You like to be praised or complimented when you look good or do something nice, so why not do the same for your children. Do not put your child down and do not call a child mean names. That can make children feel worthless instead of worthy. Don't be the one to scar your own children; they will have enough to go through as they face the real world, and low self-esteem is a big problem these days, so always be sure to show them love along with discipline. Follow the example of Jesus. We would not be who we are today had it not been for His love and discipline.

4. Teach your child to discipline his mind.

Romans 12:2 tells us, *"And be not conformed to this world: but be ye transformed by the renewing of your mind, that ye may prove what is that good, and acceptable, and perfect, will of God."*

II Corinthians 10:5 says, *"Casting down imaginations, and every high thing that exalteth itself against the knowledge of God and bringing into captivity every thought to the obedience of Christ."*

Colossians 3:2 says, *"Set your affection on things above, not on things on the earth."*

Through these Scriptures, God is teaching us the importance of disciplining our minds. If the mind is functioning right, then we can understand better. Listen to what the Scriptures say and obey God's Word.

Parents, I am not saying that if you love and discipline your children, they are always going to turn out the way you want them to; but please do all you can for them, because if a child—yours or mine—commits a crime, that child should do the time. If you want to keep your teenagers out of jail, invest time training them when they are young.

5. Do your part and leave the results to God.

Some children have it all—good parents and even discipline —they are taught right from wrong and raised in good, loving homes. Still, they turn out bad and the parents were left wondering, "Where did I go wrong?" Sometimes it makes no difference what you do, children choose to go the other way. Not all children will be what you desire, regardless of how you bring them up.

God was the perfect Father, yet He was so displeased with His disobedient creation that He was sorry He had made man. Mankind was simply weak and sinful. Of course, God gave all of us a second chance through His Son, the mediator between God and man. He goes before God and pleads our case, for He is our advocate and intercessor with God. Because He is so compassionate and so full of love, thankfully, through Him, we can be reconciled to God. But our children, just like us, also have the option of personal choice. Therefore, at some point, we must turn them over to God.

So far, we have been mostly dealing with early childhood, but let me say this about adolescence, the phase of childhood that leads into adulthood. Some irony exists during this stage because just about the time you get a handle on dealing with them as children, they start acting like they are all grown up, and you can't tell them a thing. Then when they ought to act mature and grown up, they revert to acting like little kids. That can be very frustrating for parents. You simply must learn to go with the flow. Be open minded, find out what the problem is, and deal with it. If they are acting like an adult about a situation, deal with them as you would an adult. You must discern how to give them what they need, but never let your child rule you; make sure you are always the one in control.

A lot of times you might be the problem and not the child, simply because you do not know how to be the parent. To be in control does not mean to be abusive to a child, but it does mean to spank appropriately when they are wrong. If you do this consistently, you will not need to do it by the time they get to be adolescents, for they will be under control.

Patiently continue praying and showing love. The Bible tell us a wise person will change, but a fool will remain the same. Trust God that since you did not teach your child to be a fool, your child may yet come to the point of choosing the way of the Lord.

"Give instruction to a wise man, and he will be yet wiser: teach a just man, and he will increase in learning." (Proverbs 9:9)

"A wise son heareth his father's instruction: but a scorner heareth not rebuke." (Proverbs 13:1)

6. Insist on obedience from your children.

Obedience and discipline go hand in hand. We must be obedient to God's Word and to Him, and He will always be there to help us in times of difficult problems. This is true for both parents and children.

Consider the problem of Daniel in the Old Testament. He and his friends were in a dilemma. But, unlike the others, he was obedient to God, because he had it in his heart to do what was right and please God. And so it is with us. Whether parent or child, we must obey God and then we will see and know that He is on our side and there to comfort and help us. That is because He cares for His children. The same is true of parents who care—they want their children to be the best they can possibly be, so they insist on obedience.

The following Scripture passages clearly teach the law of sowing and reaping. Patiently sow what you want to reap in your children's lives.

Be not deceived; God is not mocked: for whatsoever a man soweth, that shall he also reap. For he that soweth to his flesh shall of the flesh reap corruption; but he that soweth to the Spirit shall of the Spirit reap life everlasting. And let us not be weary in well doing, for in due season we shall reap if we faint not.

—Galatians 6:7-9

So then neither is he that planteth any thing, neither he that watereth; but God that giveth the increase. Now he that planteth and he that watereth are one: and every man shall receive his own reward according to his own labor.

—I Corinthians 3:7-8

But this I say, He which soweth sparingly shall reap also sparingly; and he which soweth bountifully shall reap also bountifully.

—II Corinthians 9:6

They that sow in tears shall reap in joy.

—Psalm 126:5

Even as I have seen, they that plow iniquity, and sow wickedness, reap the same.

—Job 4:8

Those that are planted in the house of the LORD shall flourish in the courts of our God.

—Psalm 92:13

Practical Applications for Parenting

1. Write down three ways you can teach your child responsibility and a plan for how you will implement these three ways in your life as a parent today.

2. Determine to praise your child at least once a day and make a list of areas to praise—obedience, character, kindness, responsibility, etc.

3. Refer to Galatians 6:7 and II Corinthians 9:6 above. What do these Scriptures teach you about the importance of sowing love, discipline, and other positive character traits in your children?

Chapter Three

The Big Lie About Discipline

Parents today are being sold a big lie that society keeps insisting is the truth. They are being told every day that any form of spanking constitutes child abuse, but that is simply not true. People who make that claim, according to the Bible and thousands of years of experience, are flat out wrong. The lie is very effective, though, because no decent person would ever want to hurt a child. However, a stark distinction exists between discipline and abuse.

Some supposed authorities claim that if you spank your children, it will affect them later in life. I can agree with that statement because later in life you will most certainly be able to tell the ones that were spanked from the ones that were not. And the ones who were not will be unruly, disobedient, and disrespectful adults. You do not have to spank all children equally, but you do have to consistently love and discipline. Let me just emphasize again that we need to recognize the difference between discipline and abuse.

Let me give a word of caution here. When you see a mark on a child, do not be quick to say "abuse." Be sure you have your facts straight. As I am sitting here writing, I have a wound on my leg that has been there for several days. I do not even know where it came from. All I know is that I felt an annoying pain one day and rubbed my hand over it to find a cut. This is not an uncommon occurrence for most people—and some people bruise far more easily than others depending on skin type. Sometimes children will lie when they are angry, and sometimes people will put words in their mouth. So be sure you know the truth before making an accusation of abuse. A wrong decision could cause many people a lot of pain or even ruin lives, and I know no one would want to be guilty of that. I know there are abusive parents, but I also know there are lying kids. A lie will finally catch up with the one who lied, but the damage may already be done by that time.

While some Scripture refers to using a rod on a child, that does not give license to scar or draw blood when disciplining a child. Any intelligent person knows this. My mother disciplined us, but we knew she loved us, and she never drew blood. I disciplined my kids out of love for them, but again, I never drew blood. Do not let your kids or anyone else stop you from utilizing appropriate discipline with the threat of child abuse allegations, but also be certain you are not guilty of child abuse. One day your children will appreciate the fact that you disciplined them.

I do not believe in abusing anything or anyone—especially a child. Discipline that causes physical harm or injury is of course unacceptable. But an undisciplined child is out of control, and that leaves the child without protection: *"He that hath no rule over his own spirit is like a city that is broken down, and without walls"* (Proverbs 25:28). Therefore, we need to get back to some of the time-honored "old school" methods that our own parents used to raise their children.

Rather than listening to the so-called experts, listen to God! I think of the profound words in the first chapter of the Book of Proverbs in the Bible: *"The fear of the Lord is the beginning of knowledge, but fools despise wisdom and instruction."* We need to be careful lest we turn our backs on the Lord and raise a generation of fools. It is crucial that we always teach children to obey the Lord and do right.

I have been around children all my life, and I do not believe they are unable to understand the need for physical discipline. I raised two children and helped my sister raise her kids and grandchildren. In addition, I was employed to help raise other children while their parents worked. I taught these children to respect me, and they still do. But that took work on my part. It required me to be consistent. I played when it was time to play and meant business when it was time to be firm. I did not leave any room for misunderstanding, and I gained their respect as a result.

To give you just one example, I once began to care for a young child. On my first day at work, the mother showed me where everything was and left. She neglected to tell me anything about the child's habits, so I bathed and fed her, then sat and held her until it was time for her nap. As soon as I had put her in her bed, she would begin to cry. But when I picked her up, she would immediately stop crying. This happened a few times, but she took her nap in the end.

When her mother came home, she asked how we got along, and I replied, "Fine 'till it was time for her nap."

"How did you get her to take a nap?"

"The only way she would go to sleep for me is that I had to give her a spanking," I replied. Today, people might be shocked by that, but they should not be. What has worked from the beginning of time still works perfectly now.

Years ago, I worked for a lady with four children ranging in age from seven to thirteen. A month before I started, their dad had been killed in a car wreck. Sometimes, the seven-year old would talk so disrespectfully to his mother that it made my blood boil; but I would walk away, saying to myself, "Let the mother handle it." However, she wouldn't take control, so I eventually put a stop to it by speaking to the child in a very firm tone—which just goes to show that physical discipline isn't always needed if children know it's an option. Time passed, and I ran into the mother at a meeting after the children were grown. We were glad to see each other, of course, but much to my surprise, she told me that her children still asked about me. Children both understand and appreciate it when parents/caregivers discipline and insist on proper behavior.

Today, far too many parents do not seem to know the difference between buying off their children and truly loving them. Perhaps you know exactly what I am talking about and have seen it with your own eyes. People buy their children expensive clothes, shoes, and other material possessions, often as a bribe for good behavior, thinking that is love. But it is not love; it is weakness. In fact, this kind of approach is the exact opposite of how God displays love. When God loves us, though He gives us good gifts, He also chastises us for our own good. Likewise, when we love our children, we will chastise them when necessary.

God is clear in Ephesians 6:1 when he says, *"Children, obey your parents in the Lord: for this is right."* Scripture also admonishes children to honor their parents so that their days will be long upon the earth. Undisciplined children will neither obey nor honor the authorities in their life—not their parents, and no other legitimate authorities God has placed over them.

It is our responsibility as parents to deliver this clear message to our children firmly, frequently, and with solemn authority: respect your elders, and listen to what they are trying to tell you for your own benefit, both now and in the future. So many parents today have unruly children because they will not be responsible for teaching them right from wrong and chastening them when they refuse. After all, it seems so much easier in the moment to just buy them expensive gifts—but I can guarantee that parents who do will reap the harmful results of that choice.

Parents, don't fall into the trap of blaming society or "the system" for your child's poor behavior. Raising your child well is your job—not society's. We all instinctively know right from wrong; we just need the will to follow through and choose to do what is right. Our world system today has made most parents afraid to exercise parental authority and physical discipline, because they fear they will be charged with child abuse. But if we do not train up our own flesh and blood, the system will eventually ruin those same children.

Parents need to assert themselves and stop rolling over and playing dead in the face of conflict with their children. They need to stop saying they cannot do anything with their children, which is a sure recipe for disaster. This position not only gives children the upper hand but is, in fact, harmful to them. Believe it or not, the average child *wants* discipline. Those who say otherwise are often highly educated people, but they offer only empty theories that are utterly useless in rearing obedient children who become honorable adults— which makes them educated fools.

So many children today are not being taught to have respect for anyone, and that is a tragedy. My mother always taught me to respect my elders. A child should learn how to respectfully address and interact with grown-ups, especially older adults. But many children today do not respect themselves or their parents; their behavior is disgraceful.

To all of you who are utilizing the "time out" and "one, two, and three" methods of discipline, you are allowing your children to use you and abuse you. And if you are honest, you know it does not work to resolve behavior issues either. Perhaps you send your child to his room with instructions to stay until given permission to come out. First, you must tell him several times before he goes. When he finally does go, he stays maybe five minutes and comes back out without waiting for anyone's permission. The child who does this may be small, but he is playing you for a fool.

My husband often took care of his four-year-old step granddaughter before we were married, and she was a real problem child. One day, he brought her with him for a visit, and I was in my kitchen when I heard all this commotion. I hurried into the living room to find the two of them boxing around like kangaroos. He could not do anything but try to keep her from hitting him. I stepped in and got her under control, and he thanked me. She had her Grandpa wrapped around her little finger, but believe it or not, she learned to respect me and even call me Grandmamma. Discipline was the key.

My son married a woman with two children, ages five and eight. The mother could not do anything with them, so she took them to a psychiatrist—but they only got worse instead of better. Those girls obeyed me, so their mom asked them why they obeyed me and not her. They told her that their grandmother loved them, but also spanked them and made them mind their manners. See what I mean? Don't tell me kids do not understand who will make them mind and who won't. They just need to know who is in command. While they sometimes will not like the moment of conflict, they will thank you later, especially once they reach adulthood.

Children being obedient to parents is all part of God's plan. You see, God wants us to live our best life. That will happen only when we obey Him. When we do not, He will discipline us. We should employ that same pattern with our children. Because we want the best for them, we love them and provide for their needs and sometimes even spoil them a little, but we must also chastise them. Proper discipline is in no way abusive to a child. I do not believe in beating children or putting them in dark places, but I do believe in properly spanking them.

Once children become teenagers, discipline changes shape. As good mothers, we must make sure our teens know that we love them, but we must stay on top of what is going on in their lives. Most teenagers go through a phase of being mouthy and moody as their bodies and hormones change, but a wise parent still insists on respect. When teens are going through difficult times in their lives, whether inside or outside the home, we must be there to listen and advise. We must be willing to develop a friendship so they will feel free to talk, but we must also maintain a relationship that is clearly parental. When they need someone to talk to, we should create opportunities to talk with them. However, we must always show respect and accept nothing less than the same in return from our children.

Today's youth have unparalleled opportunity for education and employment; with God's help, they can be anything they want to be. Tragically, despite such opportunities, most of them are worse off than ever before in terms of how they behave. Their language is foul and their behavior immoral. Many abuse drugs and alcohol and are heading for an early death. Teenage pregnancies have soared right along with the evil of abortion.

In my view, these behaviors all boil down to a chronic lack of discipline when these children were young because parents are believing the lies society is espousing. We need to embrace the Scriptural solution, which begins with getting back to basics in the home and using discipline appropriately for the purpose of rearing our children to be God-fearing, Christ-honoring adults. The following verses give clear admonitions to us about our responsibility in this area:

He that spareth his rod hateth his son: but he that loveth him chasteneth him betimes.

—Proverbs 13:24

Chasten thy son while there is hope and let not thy soul spare for his crying.

—Proverbs 19:18

Apply thine heart unto instruction, and thine ears to the words of knowledge. Withhold not correction from the child: for if thou beatest him with the rod, he shall not die. Thou shalt beat him with the rod, and shalt deliver his soul from hell. My son, if thine heart be wise, my heart shall rejoice, even mine.

—Proverbs 23:12-15

Practical Applications for Parenting

1. Were you spanked as a child? If so, how did this help you? If not, how did this hurt you?

2. Spanking is not the solution to every discipline problem. List situations where some other form of discipline would be appropriate.

3. Read the three scriptures shared at the end of this chapter. What do these scriptures tell you about the benefits of spanking your children when it is appropriate to do so?

Chapter Four

The Causes & Consequences of Too Little Discipline

As I go through life, I see so many parents who really don't have a clue how to rear their children. In this chapter, I want to share with you some of the causes and consequences of too little discipline in the life of a child.

I believe the number one cause of too little discipline is a failure to love your children as God loves us *"For no man ever yet hated his own flesh; but nourisheth and cherisheth it, even as the Lord the church."* (Ephesians 5:29) God gave everything to redeem us—and He did that because He loved us (John 3:16). Realize discipline is not only about punishing, spanking, and scolding children—it is first and foremost about loving them. You must take time to understand the child's current situation, and then be patient and firm as you apply discipline with love. Children are disruptive and disobedient because they are crying out for love.

A disobedient child is a miserable child—and that child will rebel against authority as a result. Unruly children are trying to say, "If you really loved me, you would make me do what's right. You say you cannot do anything with me, so I am going to do whatever I want to do. You have put me in control, and I am going to take advantage of it. When you learn how to parent, only then will I learn how to be an obedient child. "

"Since you say you love me but do not discipline me in any way, then, Mama and Daddy, cry your heart out, because I am crying too. Why? Because I want a parent who loves me enough to do whatever it takes to make me show honor and respect not only to my parents but to all adults. Don't give up on me! Help me!

"After you have done all you can, if I have still not learned my lesson, turn me over to God. If I live in your house and think I am too grown up to obey, put me out on my own to learn my lessons the hard way. You know that old saying: 'You have made your bed; now lie in it.' Be willing to let me lie in the bed I have made for myself without your intervention. I will probably be angry and even more rebellious for a while, but if that is what it takes for me to come to my senses, be willing to take that hard step because you love me. One day I will thank you for refusing to enable my rebellion."

Adults who suffer the consequences of their own rebellion will ultimately resent the parent who did not love them enough to take control of them when they were children and teach them obedience. I am so thankful my mother disciplined me while I was young; I know she did it because she loved me.

If you truly love your children, you will do what it takes to instill discipline in their lives when they are young.

A second cause of too little discipline is parents making excuses for disobedience. I often hear, "Well, these are the nineties." It is true that I have never seen so much corruption in my entire life as I see now—gangs, violence, rape, killing, and hatred are rampant. It makes no difference what culture we are from; so many of our children's problems stem from the fact that they see and hear so much hate every single day—and children tend to mimic what they see and hear. That is why we see young teens using profane language, sexually acting out as preteens and teens, and dressing as though they are looking to prostitute themselves.

However, living in a wicked world does not mean parents are absolved from the responsibility of providing a good example for their children to follow—and insisting on obedient behavior.

Moreover, stop using the excuse that you are simply unable to control your children; if I could not do anything with my child, I surely would not say it in front of my child. Children take advantage of what they hear their parents say and publicizing a child's poor behavior often makes the problem worse. Children want attention—and if the only attention they can get is because you are talking about their bad behavior, then they will act out even more to get that attention.

Parents, it is crucial for you to know and understand the difference between love and weakness. For example, so many times I will be in a store and a parent will be there with a two or three-year-old child running all over the place picking up things while the parent is chasing them around trying in vain to stop them. They catch up to their child and tell him or her to sit down and behave themselves. However, the child will jump up and say no. In frustration, the parent repeats, "I said sit down" but the child stills refuses to cooperate. Then the parent looks at some other adult (usually someone accompanying them) and just shakes their head sadly.

When you see that, you have just witnessed one of the biggest mistakes a parent can make. One of the first and most basic steps in teaching children discipline is to let them know that when you say no you mean no. It is a disgrace for a two or three-year-old to raise a hand and draw back to hit a parent, and when a parent puts up with such behavior, that parent is not showing love. Such a response is weakness.

When you love someone, all you want is for that person to be the best. You want your children to be the kind of kids' others enjoy being around, because it is clear they are on the right path to becoming good adults. Well, it is hard to like a brat, and what you think is "cute" probably makes others puke. Love without discipline is not love at all. Stop making excuses for your child.

It is never too early to train your children that respect is not optional—but that it is instead an absolute requirement. Let me tell you, if you do not demand respect from a child at the ages of two and three, then you might as well forget it. If you cannot control a two or three-year-old, you surely are not ready for older children. Listen, parents, your children *want* you to keep them in order. Now some of them will go down a bad path no matter what you do, but at least you taught them the truth when they were young. That means they may stray, but they will likely return to their upbringing in the end. But, please, regardless of the situation, do not take this kind of garbage from your children. If timeouts or "one, two, three" works, then that is fine; but you must be sure to let them know you are in charge and will handle the situation more forcefully if needed.

If you cannot control your child, it is your responsibility to figure out how to get that job done. Seek help if you need to, but never just throw up your hands in despair and quit trying.

Too little discipline is often a result of fractured families and guilt-ridden parenting. While there are numerous reasons why children become disobedient, there are also many ways you can prevent serious misbehavior from happening in the first place. For example, if possible, keep your children together. Fractured homes lead to broken children—which makes disobedience and rebellion so much more likely. Sometimes parents let other realities take a child away from them, and that can often mean a very difficult upbringing for the child.

It is usually best for siblings to be raised together, and it is good to teach them to love one another and know that whether they live at Buckingham Palace or in the ghetto, they can make a difference in each other's lives.

When families are fractured, parents are often reluctant to firmly discipline because of their guilt over the family situation. The fact is, a lot of parents are their own children's problem, especially when they did not raise those children themselves. They feel they must put up with anything the children do to prove that they do indeed love them, but that is not love; that is guilt and weakness. When we truly love our children, we demand they be respectful to us, others, and themselves. They are waiting for you to take control—and hoping deep down inside that you will, even if they do not realize it or can't put it into words.

If you were not brought up by your parents, do not take it out on your own kids, and if you did not raise your kids until later in life, don't let guilt control you. Instead, just be sure that you discipline them in the right way. A small child acts according to what he sees and hears. That is why it is so important for parents to love, discipline and serve as role models in the early days of a child's life.

Remember, you had better be on your toes because children will try you. And when they do, it is time for them to see that you are in control and have what it takes to handle their disobedience. Parents, do the best you can. If you believe in God and trust in Him, He will provide for your family's needs. Trust Him!

Too little discipline results when the authorities in a child's life are not on the same page. One day I went into a store, and some other people were there with their kids. I saw a grandmother, the mother, and several children, one of whom was being very naughty; it seemed the mother had left that child with the grandmother. When the grandmother started to discipline him, the mother came back and told the child to say, "Grandmother, don't you hit me." Bad idea! Two adults should never disagree about how to discipline a child in the presence of the child. This will cause the child to misbehave even more because they know one of you will be on their side. They notice every little exchange and will tell you, "You had better not bother me, or I will tell my mother (father, grandmother, etc.)", or whoever they think will take up for them. They will play one parent against the other, and if you take part in their little game, they will sit back and laugh at you behind your back—and if you're not careful, maybe even to your face if you continue down that road. But as the old saying goes, you had better nip it in the bud right then and there before it is too late. At first, they will take an inch, but before you know it, they will take a mile, or even two.

We as parents need to find out the whole story and not just what our child tells us because that child could be lying. Children know when they can hoodwink their parents—they are extremely intelligent about that from a very young age. In other words, they can blind and deceive us, because they know we will believe whatever they say. Though they would take advantage of us, we must ask God to lead and guide and give us wisdom to find the truth as we rear our children.

Practical Applications for Parenting

1. Do you feel guilty about an area of your life as a parent that makes you hesitant to discipline? If so, what Scripture tells you that this way of thinking is opposed to God's Word? What should you tell yourself instead when those guilt-ridden thoughts come to mind?

2. Is there another authority figure in your child's life that is not on the same page with you regarding how to discipline your child? If so, think of specific instances where this has negatively affected your child's behavior. Plan to discuss this with that authority so the two of you can work out a solution for your child's good.

3. Proverbs 3:12 and Hebrews 12:6 tell us the Lord disciplines those He loves and chastens those He accepts as sons. According to these passages, what does it demonstrate to your children when you discipline them? When you are not willing to discipline your children, what are you conveying about your love for them?

Epilogue

As we read in the Bible, a good mother watches over her household and does not eat the bread of idleness. She cherishes her children and gives them her love, and they in return rise and call her blessed. They have no doubt in their mind that she loves them, so they strive to make her proud of them. Such a wonderful relationship flourishes when parents and children can bond properly. Let's give our children praise when they deserve it. Do not put them down every time you open your mouth. A child has feelings just like we do, and although they do not always use it, they also have a brain and understand what they are taught. Children are still developing mentally, so they grasp and absorb new concepts like a sponge. What they learn will come either from a parent or from the influences of the outside world. We as parents are the ones who make that choice.

We must set goals for our kids and hope for the best. Better yet, they must set goals for themselves and not be satisfied until they have accomplished at least some of them. If you try to help yourself, someone will see you trying and lend you a helping hand. A winner never stops wanting to win. A quitter never even has a chance to win. Anything that is handed down to you on a silver platter is worthless. On the other hand, strong Christian values passed down from one generation to the next are worth more than all the gold and silver in the world combined.

Not a day goes by that I do not think about all the things my mother used to tell me. So many things she would tell me did not mean anything to me at the time, because I was young and did not take it seriously. Now, I understand so much more clearly what she was trying to convey. The discipline she exercised in my life because of her love for me was good for me, and the same is true for any child. My mother lives on, for her discipline has made me strong. Now I realize how much better it would have been if I had learned every lesson she taught while I was young. My life has benefited in so many ways because she was a loving and caring mother who insisted on my obedience even when I did not understand. She brought me up right, and I am so thankful to her for always being there for me.

It makes me sick to see what kind of society we are living in, and oh how disappointed God must be with us, to show such little respect for all that He and His Son have done and are still constantly doing for us. It hurts me deeply to see so much sin in some of our children's lives.

I know that not all parents who don't go to church are bad, but it's better if two people (in this instance I mean a parent and child) share common ground, and the main thing they need to have in common is Jesus. If a parent and child both know and accept Him as their personal Savior, they can pray for God's help in all the situations that arise in parenting.

So, as a father or mother, but most of all as a child of the Most High King, we must let our lives be acceptable to God so that we can serve as role models for our children and tell them about the Living Water from a well that never runs dry.

However, if you are the parent of a rebellious teenager, it is not too late for God to turn their life around. Start by teaching them to be obedient to their parents and elders. If they feel they have been mistreated, help them turn the negative around into a positive. And most importantly, ask God to help you. He will give you the strength and patience you will need. And never forget that change is possible with the tools of love and discipline. It worked for my mama. It worked for me. And it will work for you too.

Concluding Thoughts: Trusting God in Hard Times

Praise God for deliverance! II Samuel 22:2-3 says, *"The Lord is my rock and my fortress and my deliverer; the God of my strength, in whom I will trust."* He is our everything and will be there to help us. He is our protector and will lead and guide us if we have faith in Him. He will keep us from the strong enemy that is trying to destroy us. We must do as Daniel and put the Lord in first place in our hearts.

Life is a struggle for most people, with or without children. However, nothing worthwhile ever comes easily;

reaching a goal requires hard work, and sometimes we still do not make it, but we must keep on trying. Defeat is when we give up and quit, but Mama said you do not know what you can do till you give it your best shot.

As I mentioned at the beginning of this book, when I first began to think about writing a book, I was going to write poems, songs and stories and have them published. And I did write, but I never tried to get anything published. I would always say that I did not know how to get in touch with a publisher, but that was just an excuse. I was not really trying. Once I decided to write on this topic, I realized how difficult it was to write, and I came to a complete stop more than once. Sometimes days or weeks would pass before I started writing again, but I was determined to finish, for though quitters never finish, a finisher never quits. Writing the book was a kind of discipline for me, because I knew my mama was saying, "Rene, you can do it." Keeping God first and remembering how she loved and disciplined me was a motivation for me to realize that I not only could finish the book but wanted to finish it.

It has taken long hours, tired eyes, patience, love, and stress to write this book. Most of all, it took God's love and guidance, because all along He was with me all the way, and He is a mighty good leader. As hard as it has been, though, it has also been a joyous experience for me because I feel like someone is going to take heed to my message and be helped. I have let God lead me all the way, and I have tried to speak as honestly as possible—even when I might have seemed hard. It is my hope this book helps you to be the parent God created you to be.

Prayers & Prose

The following is a collection of prayers and prose that I have compiled throughout the writing of this book. Perhaps you will find something here to help you develop your own prayers as a parent to a heavenly Father who loves you and wants the very best for you and your children.

Thank you, God, for letting Your Son die on the cross for me and for the whole world. Thank You for life, health, and strength. Thank you for a new day that was not promised to me. Thank you for my children. But most of all, thank you for raising your Son from the dead so we can all be part of the royal family of God and joint heirs with Christ. Amen.

Lord, we want to thank you for the knowledge through education that you have given us. We thank you for our hard struggle, that we may learn how to depend more on You. We thank you for showing us love. Although we ourselves have been undisciplined at times, just as our children are, you still love us. We thank you for showing us how to be parents, so that we may love our children while still disciplining them— as you do us. We thank you because all kids are not out of control. We thank you for giving us understanding. We thank you for being so patient with us so we can learn how to be patient with our loved ones. We thank you for the ability to be concerned about others in our lives, not just our own family. Lord, I personally thank you for giving me the strength and mind to keep the faith, and the courage to keep on going because it surely has not been easy. As I always say, I am sure it wasn't easy for you up there on the cross either, but you stayed there even when you were innocent, and I'm guilty. But you still love me, and I thank you from the bottom of my heart, for through your love I have learned how to endure. Amen.

Lord, the Most Holy One, please forgive us for our many sins. Oh, Lord, I hope all will come to the knowledge, if we want to do better and have a sincere heart, you are waiting for us to ask you for Your help. And then and only then will You give us the strength. Oh, Lord, we are not looking for an easy way out, but we need a little more faith. Lord, as I write and pray this prayer, I know from experience that life is not easy. But if we keep the faith and trust in you, it will get better at your appointed time. Thank You, dear Jesus, for giving us an opportunity to have everlasting life. Amen.

Father, we thank You for being so patient with us and showing such love. There has never been such great love as yours, and, Father, your love has taught me how to love. I thank you for sharing your love with whoever will accept it. Amen.

🙏

Thank You, Lord, for Your eternal love. I do not deserve it but thank You anyway. Amen.

🙏

Dear God, Thanks for leading and guiding me. Thank you for teaching me how to be disciplined and obedient, and, dear God, I want to be more like your Son, Jesus, who gave His life for me. Please do not ever let it all be in vain. Lord, I love You. Amen.

Lost Child

I am a lost child that can't find my way

Oh God, will You please help me today?

Mama taught me and showed me what was right and what
was wrong

I did not listen and take heed to what she said

And now I realize I am a lost child who has lost my way

Oh, God, will you please help me today?

For I have strayed far away

But now I want to let you lead the way

Thank you, God, and Mama too

This lost child knows now what to do.

Discipline Me

Discipline me. Discipline me if you must

Don't do it because I am a child and can't make a fuss

But because I am your child and you love me so much

And I really do want to understand such

Be patient with me and do what you must do

And maybe one day I will understand discipline too

For right now I am a child doing whatever you let me do

You have told me and I know it for myself too

That you rule and in your own way are doing whatever you

have to do

And while showing me your patience, compassion, and love

Show me your discipline too.

Because I Really Care

Dear children, I love you all

I don't want you to fail or fall

Sorry that you think I'm so unfair,

That's because I really care

If you need me to help, I will take that step

Please always remember, life is not always fair

I love you a lot; maybe one day you will take my spot

I know you understand why there is such demand

News here and news there; a little news everywhere

Even if it's hard for you to say, I know you love me anyway

Oh, come and walk a little way with me

And then you will be able to see

It's no lie; this world is out of control

There are not a lot of good models or roles

Everybody seems to be doing their own thing

As if no one cares. God help us

For only you know where the end will be

For the boys and girls of today and history

We as parents just hope one day

Our children will understand

And follow your plan.